Heal Me Lord, with Prayer

Ingrid D Stubbs

WESTBOW·
PRESS
A DIVISION OF THOMAS NELSON
& ZONDERVAN

Scripture taken from the New King James Version. Copyright © 1979, 1980,
1982 by Thomas Nelson, Inc. Used by permission. All rights reserved.

Scripture taken from the Holy Bible, NEW INTERNATIONAL VERSION®.
Copyright © 1973, 1978, 1984 by Biblica, Inc. All rights reserved worldwide.
Used by permission. NEW INTERNATIONAL VERSION® and NIV® are
registered trademarks of Biblica, Inc. Use of either trademark for the offering
of goods or services requires the prior written consent of Biblica US, Inc.

Scripture quotations taken from the Holy Bible, New Living Translation,
Copyright © 1996, 2004. Used by permission of Tyndale House
Publishers, Inc., Wheaton, Illinois 60189. All rights reserved.

WestBow Press books may be ordered through booksellers or by contacting:

WestBow Press
A Division of Thomas Nelson & Zondervan
1663 Liberty Drive
Bloomington, IN 47403
www.westbowpress.com
1 (866) 928-1240

Because of the dynamic nature of the Internet, any web addresses or
links contained in this book may have changed since publication and
may no longer be valid. The views expressed in this work are solely those
of the author and do not necessarily reflect the views of the publisher,
and the publisher hereby disclaims any responsibility for them.

Any people depicted in stock imagery provided by Thinkstock are models,
and such images are being used for illustrative purposes only.
Certain stock imagery © Thinkstock.

ISBN: 978-1-4908-9141-5 (sc)
ISBN: 978-1-4908-9142-2 (e)

Print information available on the last page.

WestBow Press rev. date: 08/11/2015

CONTENTS

Acknowledgements

This book is dedicated to my present pastors, Pastor Tony Townsend and First Lady Liz Townsend. One day, my Pastor said, "You are an intercessor." At that moment I finally understood why I was always drawn to pray for others both openly and privately. Pastor Tony told me he wanted me to open up our Sunday morning service with prayer for the children on a regular basis.

On a separate occasion, my First Lady, Liz said, "You are called to alter ministry. Get ready and prepare yourself." She also gave me a prophetic word that said the Word of God is inside me, I know the Word, and I should use God's Word, not only for writing my poems but to pray for and help others. I thank God for my pastors speaking into my life, believing in me, and always having my back. Many blessings to them, their children, their extended family, and Faith Community Church family in York, Pennsylvania.

I also want to thank my mother and father, my husband George and sons Zephaniah and Nehemiah for their love, support, and encouragement.

Introduction

In January 2013, the Lord spoke to me about writing several books. I immediately embraced the idea, then after thinking about it, I said, "who me?" My initial ideas were for a daily devotional, a book of prayer, and an ongoing book of poems, and a children's book.

The year went by with many challenges such as, limited time, insufficient storage space on my computer, distractions, finances, and prioritizing. I worked diligently on the daily devotional but I missed the deadline to have it hit the stores by October of that year. I then heard clearly from the Lord that I was to work on the book of prayer.

I was not sure which publisher to use. I called our assistant pastor, Elder Marshall Leonard, for wisdom and prophetic insight, and he said he would go before the Lord and call me back within an hour. He called me back within fifteen minutes and said, "The publisher I was talking with was the right one for you." I received total peace about the decision, so today I'm working with CrossBooks.

ANGER

He who is slow to anger is better than the mighty, and he who rules his spirit than he who takes a city.

—Proverbs 16:32

PRAYER

Father, in the name of Jesus I come against the spirit of anger; it is not of You. As I give it to You, You are filling me with Your peace and Your joy and Your love. I give You all of my pains, hurts, and fears because You care for me and You love me; I am Yours.

I thank You that anger will no longer rule my life; I am free, I am released, and I am delivered in Jesus' name. I bind the generational curse of anger and break it off my life, my children's lives, and my entire family.

In Jesus' mighty name. Amen.

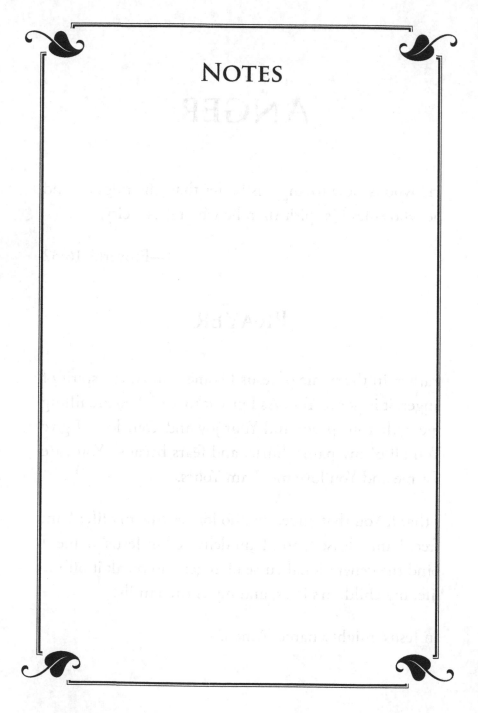

NOTES

BITTERNESS

And she was in bitterness of soul, and prayed to the Lord and wept in anguish.

—1 Samuel 1:10

PRAYER

Lord, I am coming to You to help me remove the bitterness that is deep down in my soul because I was wronged. Help me to see others as You see them and remove all bitterness from within me. Please do not let it block my blessings and stop me from accomplishing Your plan for my life. Make me sweet and loving toward others as You are to me. In Jesus' miraculous name. Amen

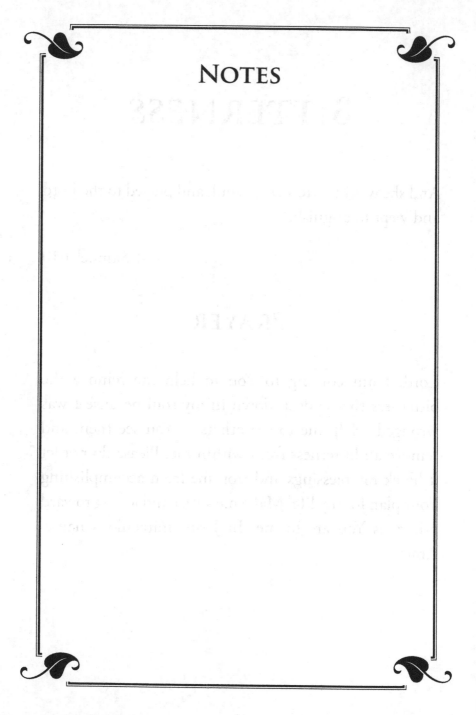

NOTES

CARES

And the cares of this world, the deceitfulness of riches, and the desires for other things entering in choke the Word, and it becomes unfruitful.

—Mark 4:19 (read verses 4:13–20)

PRAYER

Father, I cast all my cares on You because You care for me. My eyes are fixed on You and Your ways and not what is going on in my life. Thank You, Lord, for taking every care from me. I am not equipped to carry it. I bind every worry, concern, fear, and anxiety from manifesting in my life. Let Your Word grow freely in me that I may become a fruitful vessel for Your Kingdom! In Jesus' mighty name. Amen!

NOTES

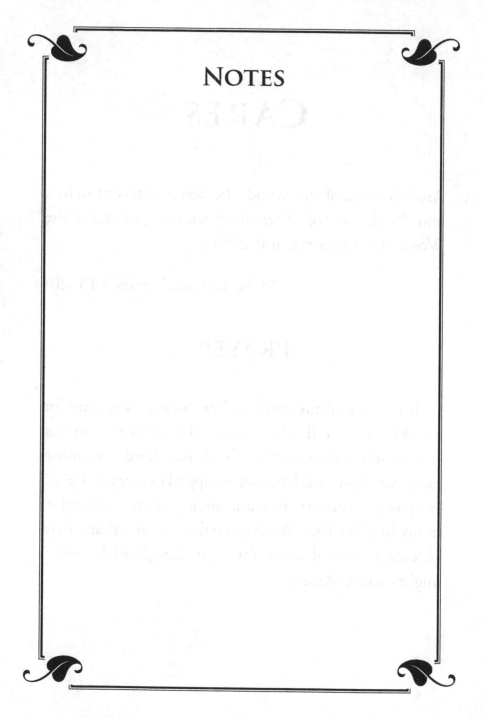

CHILDREN

You shall love the Lord with all your heart, with all your soul, and with all your strength. And these words which I command you today shall be in your heart. You shall teach them diligently to your children, and shall talk of them when you sit in your house, when you walk by the way, when you lie down, and when you rise up.

— Deuteronomy 6:5–7

PRAYER

Lord, I thank You for my children; they are a gift from You. Help me to teach them and train them in Your way. Protect them wherever they go. Help my children to be obedient to all authority. Let Your word be in their hearts and give them a holy boldness to share You with their generation. I cancel every trap the devil has set for them. We thank you God that our children are the future and Your will for their lives shall come to pass. In Jesus' wonderful name, Amen.

NOTES

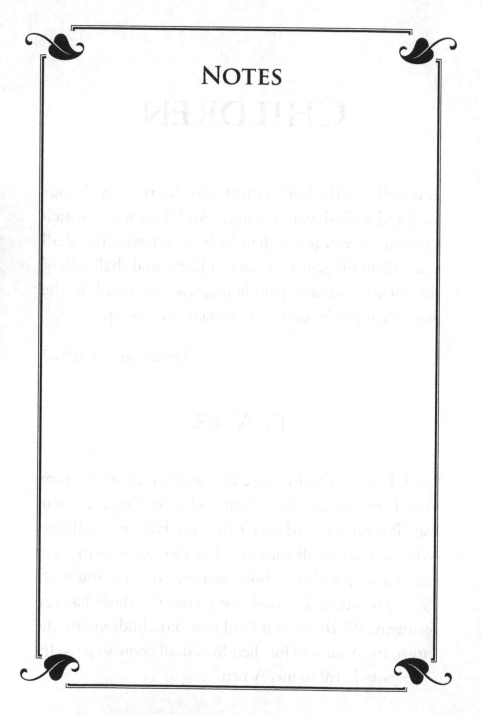

Disappointments

And we know that all things work together for good to those who love God, to those who are the called according to His purpose.

—Romans 8:28

Prayer

Father, thank You for turning all disappointments around and making them into something good for me. Help me to always see Your blessings even when things are not going my way. I will focus on Your Word, which will bring life to all my circumstances. I love You, and I thank You that every disappointment is an opportunity to trust You even more, Lord. In Jesus' magnificent name, Amen!

NOTES

ENCOURAGEMENT

That their hearts may be encouraged, being knit together in love, and attaining to all riches of the full assurance of understanding, to the knowledge of the mystery of God, both of the Father and of Christ, in whom are hidden all the treasures of wisdom and knowledge.

—Colossians 2:2–3

PRAYER

Lord, I thank You that You encourage me moment by moment, and I have assurance in You and Your Word, as You reveal the love You have for me. Thank You for giving me wisdom and understanding about my situations. Help me to encourage others as You encourage me. In Jesus' wonderful name, Amen.

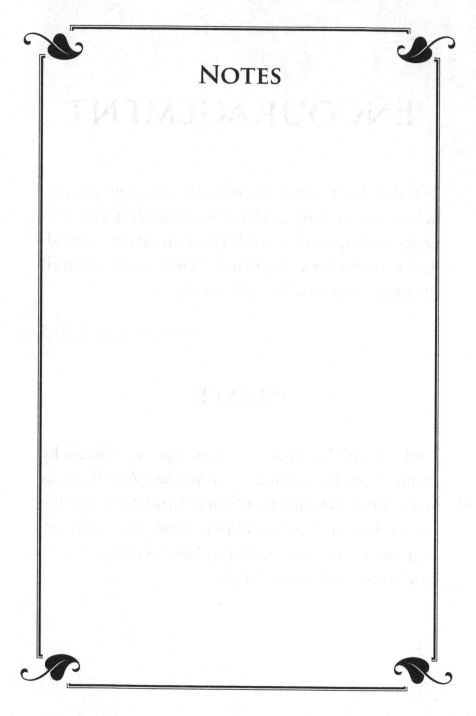

NOTES

FAILURE

For I know the thoughts that I think towards you, says the Lord, thoughts of peace and not of evil, to give you a future and a hope.

— Jeremiah 29:11

PRAYER

Lord, my failures do not define me. Failures might just mean "not now." Thank You for having good thoughts toward me, having a future for me, and allowing me to have hope in You. Thank You, Lord, for seeing me as a success and not a failure. I also thank You for seeing me as a winner, no matter what I go through. In Jesus name, Amen!

NOTES

GUIDANCE

In all your ways acknowledge Him, and He shall direct your paths.

—Proverbs 3:6

PRAYER

Father, I need Your guidance for my life and the decisions I make. I thank You for directing me because I cannot make it on my own. My heart cries out to You, Lord. Help me to stay on Your straight and narrow path of righteousness, not looking to the left nor looking to the right, but looking to You always. All my answers are in You, not the people or the circumstances. In Jesus' precious name, Amen!

NOTES

HURTS

I waited patiently for the Lord; and He incline to me, and heard my cry.

—Psalm 40:1

PRAYER

Lord, I cry out to You. I know You are my healer, and I give You every hurt and pain, physically and emotionally. Thank You for hearing my cry and healing every hurt. Father, I forgive those who have hurt me. There is no hurt that is too great for You to heal. Thank You for touching my innermost being so I may begin my healing process. In Jesus' precious name, Amen!

NOTES

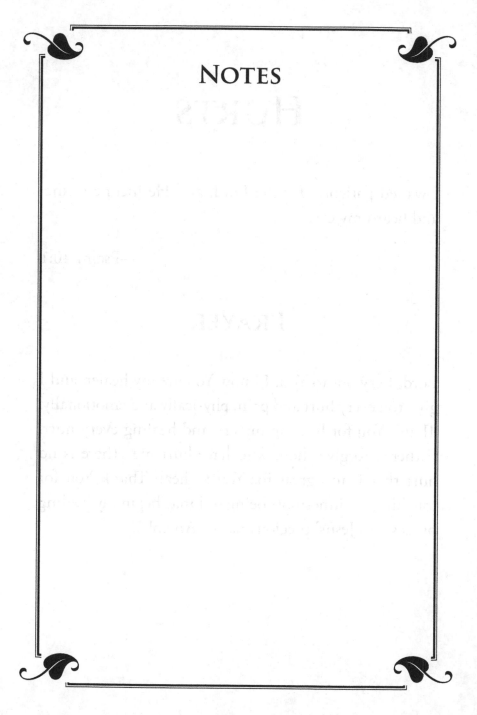

INTERCESSION

Therefore He is also able to save to the uttermost those who come to God through Him, since He always lives to make intercession for them.

—Hebrews 7:25

PRAYER

Lord, I thank You for interceding on my behalf. I don't have to carry it all by myself. You are there for me. When the Devil accuses me, You are standing in the gap for me. Help me to intercede for others also. In Jesus' matchless name, Amen.

NOTES

JOBS

But if anyone does not provide for his own, and especially for those of his household, he has denied the faith and he is worse than an unbeliever.

—1 Timothy 5:8

PRAYER

Lord, thank You for my job so I can provide for my family. Help me to be a light in my workplace. I pray for blessings for the company, CEO, and all management and supervisors, that You may lead them and guide them.

I bind up every spirit of darkness, immorality, hostility, jealousy, backbiting, sexual sins, and discrimination. I release a spirit of holiness, love, peace, and joy in the workplace. Thank You, Lord, that I am not conforming to the ways of the world but am transforming daily that others may see the light of God in me. Thank You for presenting opportunities for me to reach the lost on my job.

In Jesus' excellent name, Amen.

NOTES

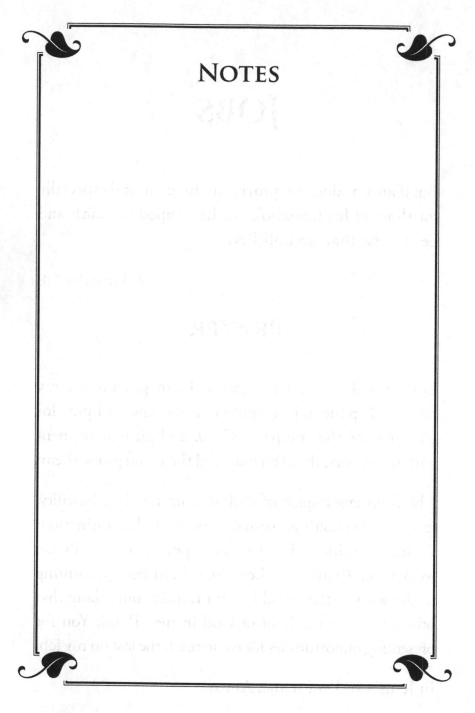

KINDNESS

But when the kindness and the love of God our Savior toward man appeared, not by works of righteousness which we have done, but according to His mercy He saved us, through the washing of regeneration and renewing of the Holy Spirit, whom He poured out on us abundantly through Jesus Christ our Savior, that having been justified by His grace we should become heirs according to the hope of eternal life.

—Titus 3:4–7

PRAYER

Lord, teach me Your character so I can be more like You. I thank You for Your kindness toward me, that You do not look at my faults. I can rejoice that Your grace and mercy has been given to me and I am an heir of Your Kingdom. Fill my heart with kindness toward others. In Jesus' wonderful name, Amen!

NOTES

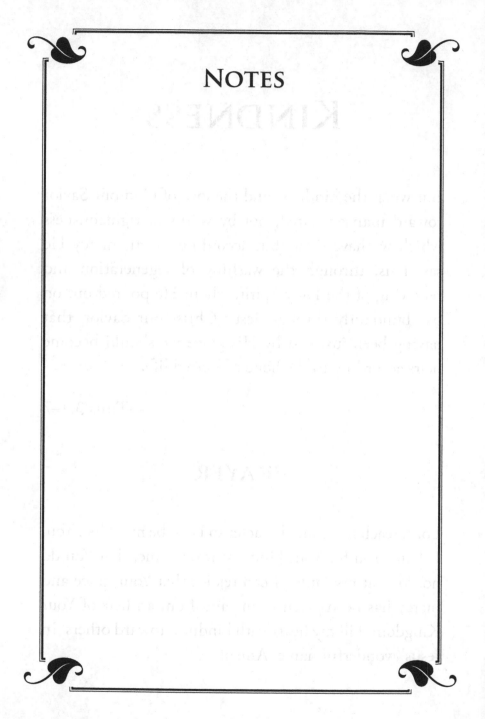

LOVE

He who does not love does not know God, for God is love. In this the love of God was manifested towards us, that God has sent His only begotten Son into the world, that we might live through Him.

1 John 4:8–9

PRAYER

Lord, teach me to love like You do—unconditionally. Your love is unmeasurable, it is gracious, it is wonderful and fulfilling. Your love is great! Remind me daily of Your love toward me—that You gave Your only begotten Son to die for me so I may have eternal life with You. Help me to love the unlovable so that others will see You in me and know I belong to *You*.

I declare and decree that I will love others into the kingdom, by seeing them through the eyes of God.

In Jesus' precious name, Amen!

Notes

MONEY

No one can serve two masters. For you will hate one and love the other, or be devoted to one and despise the other. You cannot serve both God and money.

—Matthew 6:24 (NLT)

PRAYER

Dear Lord, let me serve You with my whole heart, pleasing You in all that I do. Help me not serve money by chasing after it, comprising my integrity and holiness, or putting money before You. Yes, money is needed to survive in this world, but You are needed more than anything money can buy. I give You all my needs, and I know they will be met. You hold all resources in Your hands. In Jesus' mighty name, Amen!

NOTES

Nothing without God

I am the vine, you are the branches. He who abides in Me, and I in him, bears much fruit; for without Me you can do nothing.

—John 15:5

Prayer

Father, as a child of God, I am connected to You and Your Word. As I get in Your presence and study Your Word, You are teaching me and leading me to help reach others for Your Kingdom. Lord, without You I can do nothing. Help me to remain connected to You. In Jesus' name, Amen!

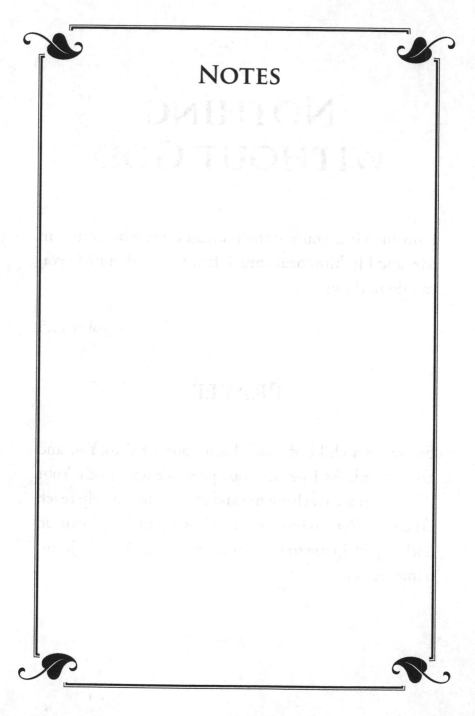

NOTES

Oppression

The Lord also will be a refuge for the oppressed, a refuge in times of trouble.

—Psalm 9:9

Prayer

Father, we know that oppression is from the devil to keep us down and from fulfilling our purpose. We bind up every spirit of oppression and depression and cast it back into the pit of hell. I dismantle every scheme to keep oppression in my life. Every chain is loosened now, in Jesus' name. It will no longer keep me bound. Lord, we thank You for being our refuge in times of trouble to lift us up and heal us from all oppression. In Jesus' mighty name, Amen.

NOTES

PASSION

And being in Bethany at the house of Simon the leper, as He sat at the table, a woman came having an alabaster flask of very costly oil of spikenard. Then she broke the flask and poured it on His head. But there were some who were indignant among themselves, and said, "Why was this fragrant oil wasted"? For it might have been sold for more than three hundred denarii and given to the poor. And they criticized her sharply. But Jesus said, "let her alone. Why do you trouble her? She has done a good work for Me."

—Mark 14:3-6

PRAYER

Father, in the name of Jesus, our passions and desires come from You. You have placed them in our hearts to be used for Your glory. Therefore, others will see and not understand. Lord, help me to pursue all You have given me so You may be glorified. In Jesus' powerful name, Amen.

NOTES

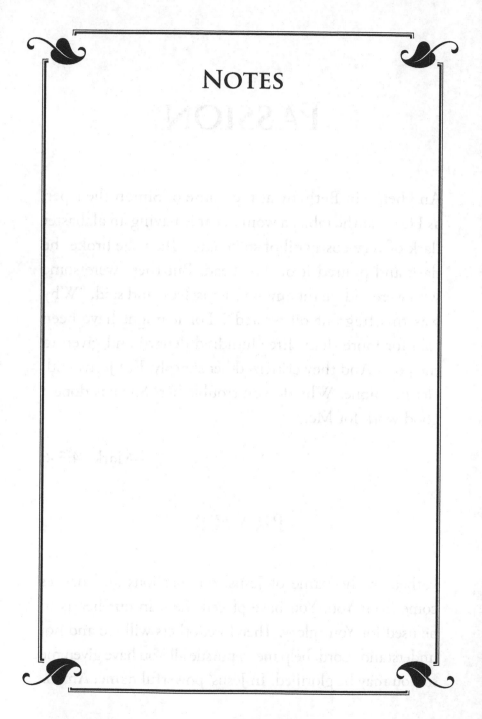

PEACE

Pursue peace with all people, and holiness, without which no one will see the Lord.

—Hebrews 12:14

PRAYER

Lord, help me daily to seek after peace with all people. It doesn't matter what our differences may be or what circumstances may arise. Father, without holiness no one will see You. We put our flesh under submission and declare peace and holiness to operate in our lives. In Jesus' name, Amen.

NOTES

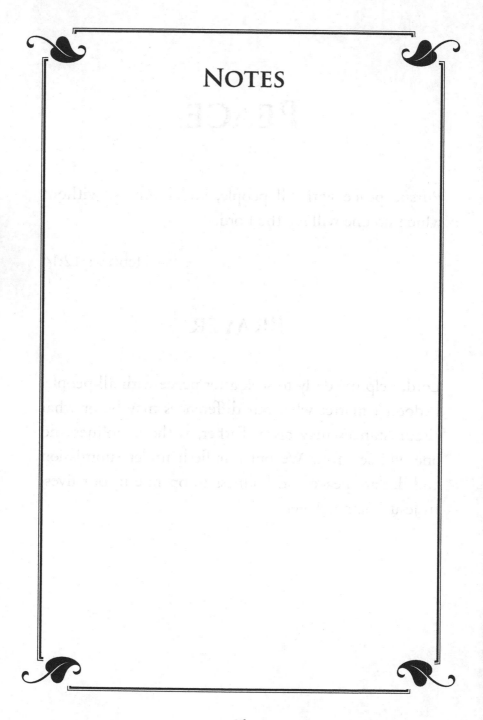

QUENCHING

Do not quench the Spirit.

—1 Thessalonians 5:19

PRAYER

Lord, the Holy Spirit has free course in my life. Help me not to stop, stifle, or quench Him. Teach me not to grieve the Holy Spirit by not trusting and relying on Him to guide me and direct me in what I should or should not do, where I should go and should not go. I need You more each day. In Jesus' name, Amen.

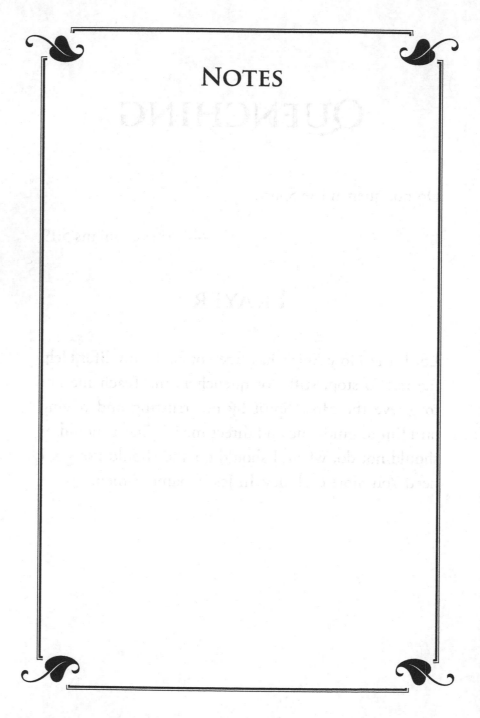

NOTES

REST

Rest in the Lord, and wait patiently for Him; do not fret because of him who prosper in his way, because of the man who brings wicked schemes to pass.

—Psalm 37:7

PRAYER

Lord, I look to You and not others who are prospering or doing wickedness. Father, I rest in You and You alone. I will wait patiently on You to make me prosper and to give me what You have placed down inside of me to bring You glory. As I rest in You, You are filling me with Your peace, and I say, "Thank You, Lord." In Jesus' marvelous name, Amen.

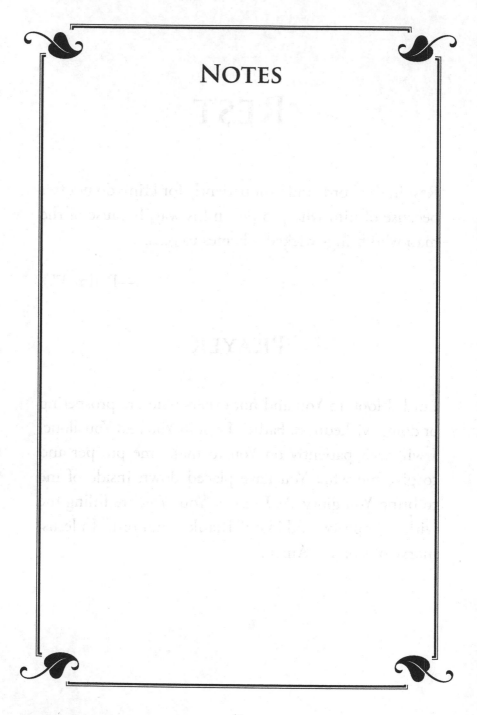

NOTES

SUBMISSIVE

Likewise you younger people, submit yourselves to your elders. Yes, all of you be submissive to one another, and be clothed with humility, for God resists the proud, but gives grace to the humble. Therefore humble yourselves under the mighty hand of God, that He may exalt you in due time.

—1 Peter 5:5–6

PRAYER

Father, I come to You in the name of Jesus with a submissive and surrendered heart. I also submit to those You have placed in my life. I humble myself before You; teach me to always walk in humility and not to be prideful or puffed up in any way. Lord, You only give grace to the humble but resist the proud. I pray that Your grace continue to rest upon me because my heart is surrendered to You. In Jesus' name, Amen.

NOTES

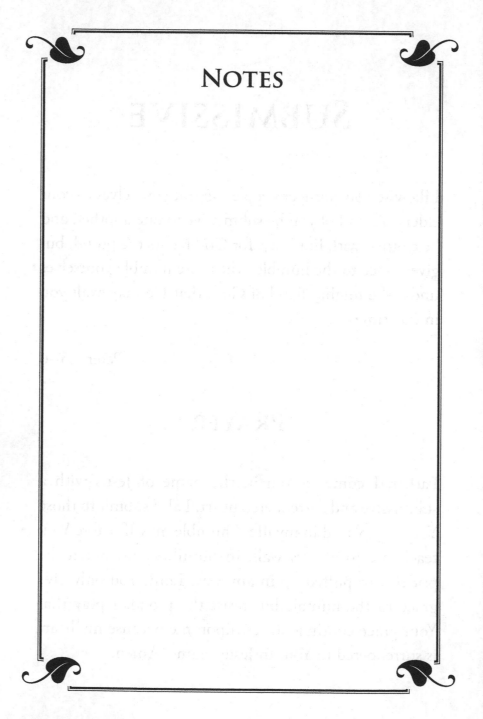

TRUST

Trust in the Lord with all your heart, and lean not on your own understanding; in all your ways acknowledge Him, and He shall direct your paths.

—Proverbs 3:5–6

PRAYER

Lord, I put my entire trust in You. My life is in Your hands; I will not trust in people. There are things that I do not understand, but You do. I acknowledge You as head over me. I do not want to make decisions without You and trusting You to direct me every step of the way. Have Your way in my life. In Jesus' amazing name, Amen.

NOTES

Understanding

Who is wise and understanding among you? Let him show by good conduct that his works are done in the meekness of wisdom.

—James 3:13

Prayer

Father, I come to You seeking understanding in areas of my life that are unclear. Fill me with wisdom and understanding of Your Word. Help me to remain humble and let everything I do and say come from You. Thank You that Your understanding is unmeasurable, even when I miss it. I thank You for Your love and understanding as I continue to follow after You. In Jesus' incredible name, Amen.

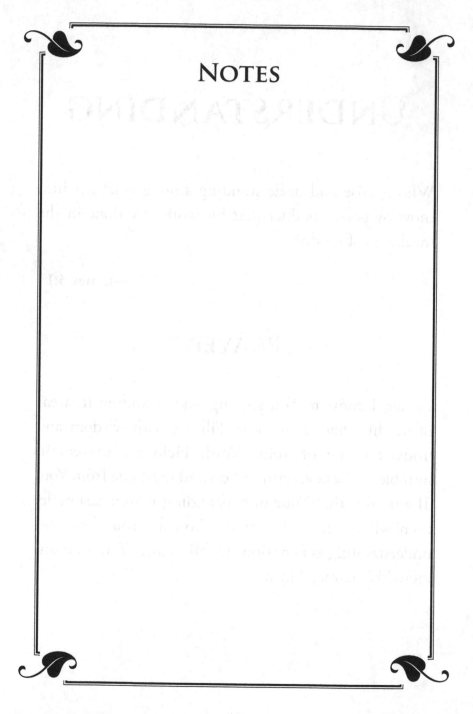

VICTORY

For every child of God defeats this evil world, and we achieve this victory through our faith. And who can win this battle against the world? Only those who believe that Jesus is the Son of God?

—1 John 5:4–5 (NLT)

PRAYER

Dear Heavenly Father, I thank You that all victory has been given to me because of Your death on the cross and Your rising on the third day. I continue to have total trust in You by using my faith. I believe Jesus is the Son of God and I have eternal life with You. I have victory over death and hell, sickness, disease, poverty, and lack. Because I have accepted You as my Lord and Savior, I am victorious in all areas of my life. In Jesus' name, Amen.

NOTES

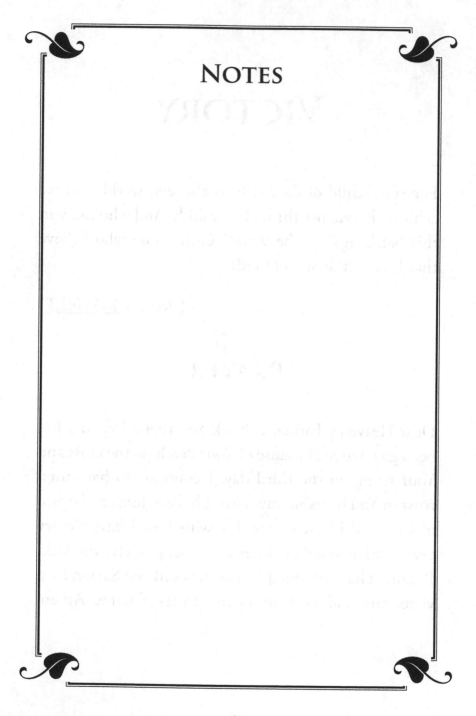

48

WILL OF GOD

Your Kingdom come. Your will be done on earth as it is in heaven.

— Matthew 6:10

PRAYER

Dear heavenly Father, we desire to have heaven here on earth, for this is Your will! I declare and decree no more sickness and disease, lack, insecurity, pain, suffering, murder, and peer pressure in our children. Father, I loose and I decree that I have health, abundance, and confidence in who I am in You and Your peace and unity in our homes, schools, neighborhoods, cities, and country. Set us free! Move on the hearts of the next generation to live for You, for this is Your will. In Jesus' mighty name, I pray. Amen!

NOTES

Xtraordinary (Extraordinary)

For you see your calling, brethren, that not many wise according to the flesh, not many mighty, not many noble, are called. But God has chosen the foolish things of the world to put to shame the wise, and God has chosen the weak things of the world to put shame the things that are mighty.

—1 Corinthians 1:26–27

Prayer

Lord, You use ordinary people to do extraordinary things for Your Kingdom. We come before You humble with forgiving hearts, demonstrating Your love to all—even those who have wronged us—our hearts surrendered to You and Your will. You can and will use us to bring about Your plan. It doesn't matter where we have been or what we have done; accepting You as our Lord and Savior wipes our slates clean, giving us a new start with You. Lord, here I am; use me to reach the dying world for You. In Jesus' precious name, Amen.

NOTES

Yearning

O God, You are my God; early will I seek You; my soul thirst for You, my flesh longs for You in a dry and thirsty land where there is no water. So I have looked for You in the sanctuary, to see Your power and Your glory.

—Psalm 63:1–2

Prayer

Dear Father, my heart longs for You. There is joy and peace in fellowship with You. Let me experience Your love in the most intimate way; there is none like You. No one can fill my heart as You do. I enter into Your presence with thanksgiving. I hunger for more of You. Oh how I need You daily; I can't make it without You, dear Lord. My soul yearns for You like water in a dessert, and I know I will be filled.

Thank You, Lord, for Your presence, Your peace, Your joy, and most of all Your love.

In Jesus' wonderful name, Amen.

NOTES

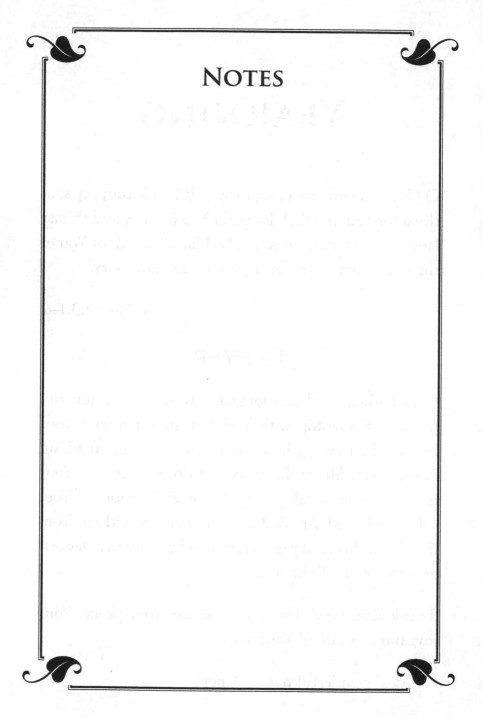

ZEAL

Rejoice in the Lord always. I will say it again: Rejoice!

—Philippians 4:4 (NIV)

PRAYER

Lord, I delight myself in You; I celebrate You. You fill me with joy, and You are my everything. You have given me eternal life with You. I surrender to You daily, declaring Your will be done in my life and those of my loved ones. Let others see the love, joy and passion I have toward You and desire to know You also. I will continue in Your ways, I thank You, I praise You, and worship You, Lord. I chase after You.

In Jesus' name, Amen!

NOTES

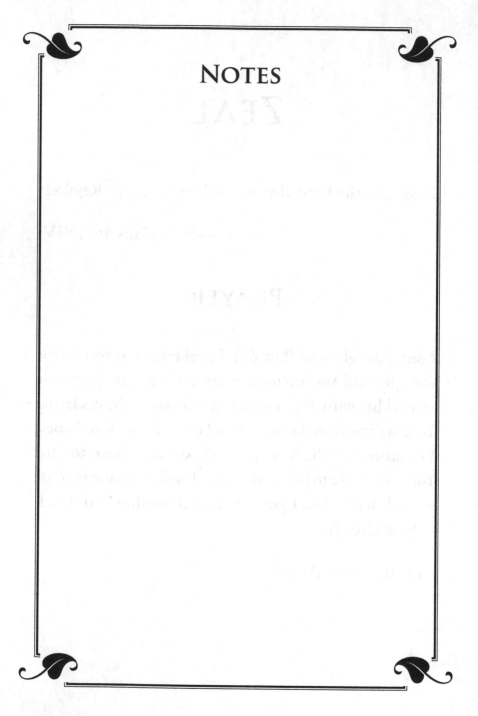

Salvation Prayer

(To receive Jesus as your Lord and Savior)

For whoever calls on the name of the Lord shall be saved.

Romans 10:13

Dear Lord Jesus,

Come into my heart. Forgive me of my sins. Cleanse me and change me. I believe God raise Jesus from the dead on the third day. I turn my back on the world and I turn my back on sin. Fill me with Your Holy Spirit and set me free. Give me a passion for the lost and a hunger for the things of God. Help me to fulfill all that You have called me to do. Thank You for forgiving me; I am saved and on my way to heaven. In Jesus' name, Amen!

Prayer changes things!

Printed in the United States
By Bookmasters